ABC animal
is one big tracing for preschoolers : Fun book to practice writing beginner to tracing half lines for toddlers

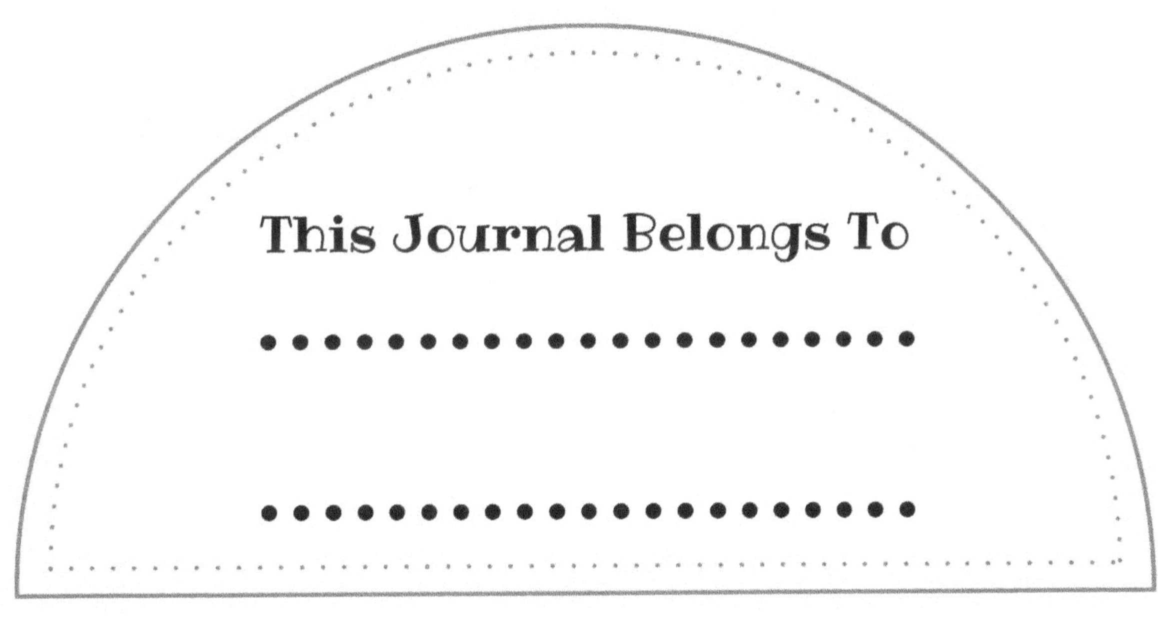

A is for Alligator

a is for Alligator

Tracing A, a, A, a

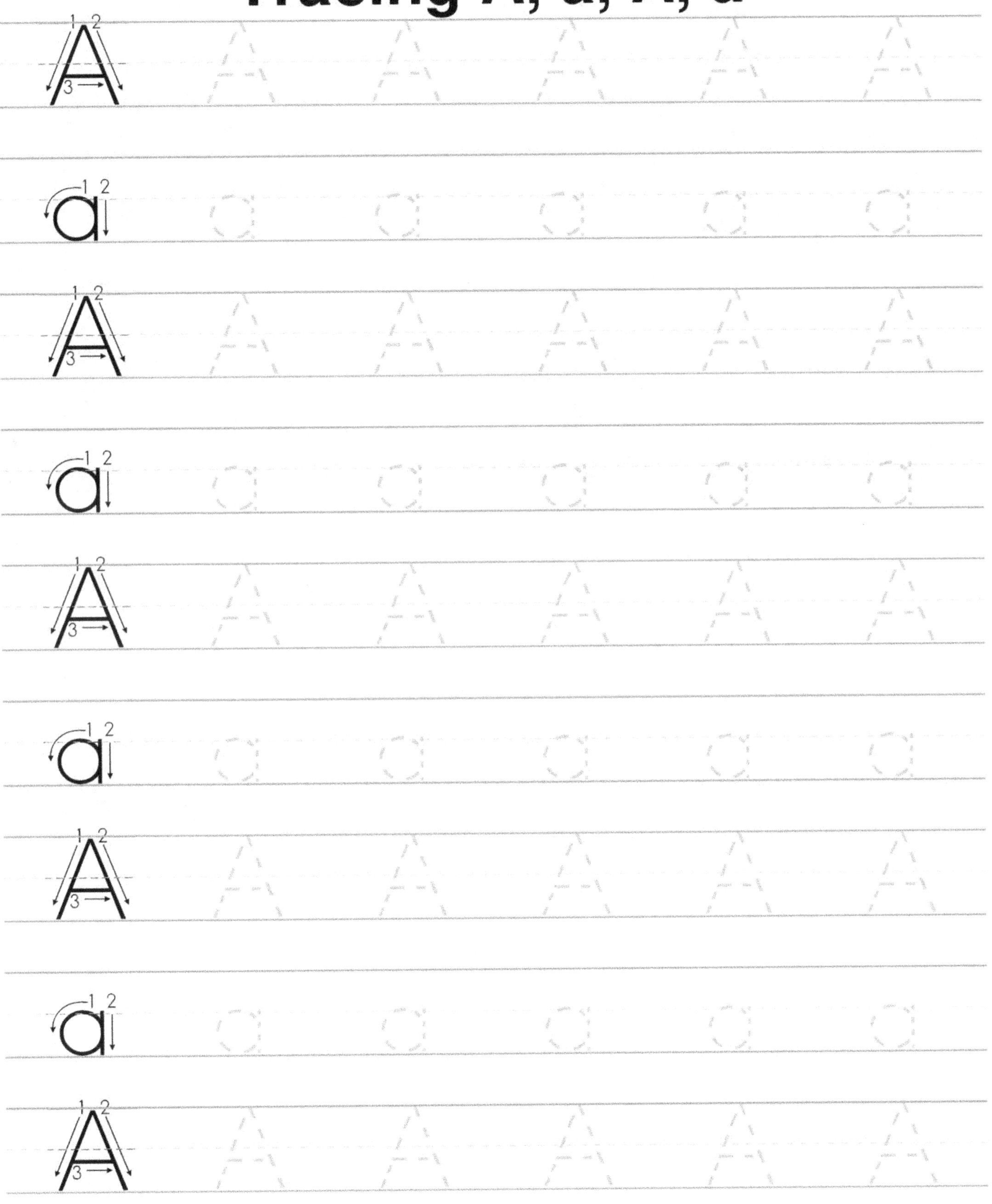

B is for Butterfly

b is for Butterfly

Tracing B, b, B, b

C is for Crab

c is for Crab

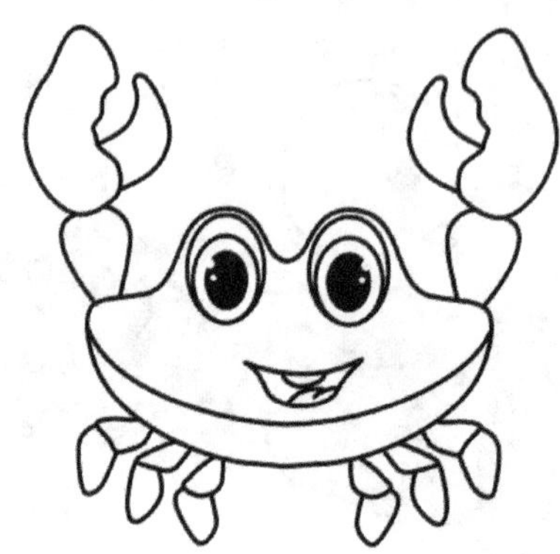

Tracing C, c, C, c

D is for Dolphin

d is for Dolphin

Tracing D, d, D, d

E is for Elephant

e is for Elephant

Tracing E, e, E, e

F is for Fish

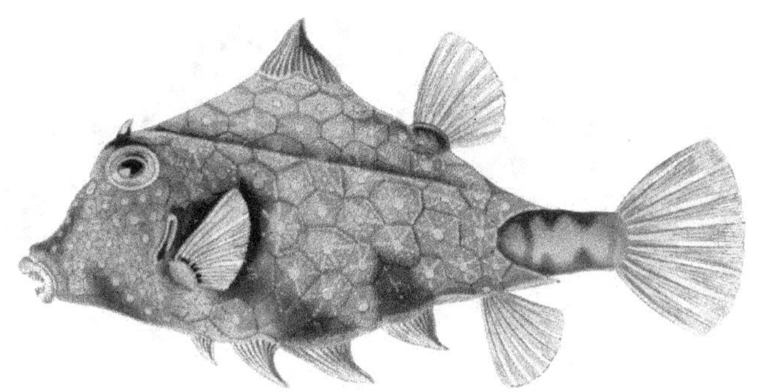

f is for Fish

f f f f f f
f f f f f f
f f f f f f
f f f f f f
f f f f f f
f f f f f f
f f f f f f

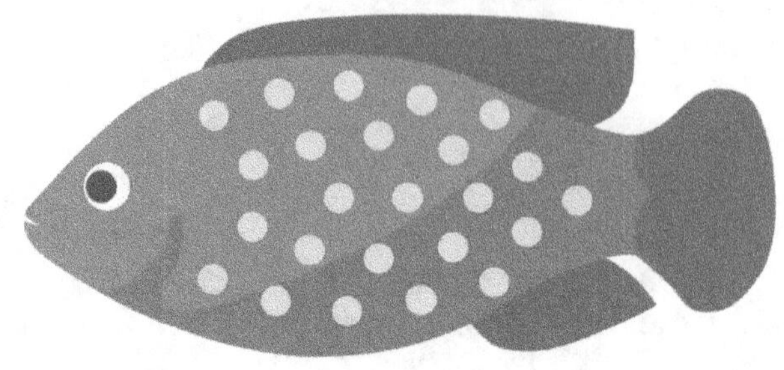

Tracing F, f, F, f

G is for Gecko

g is for Gecko

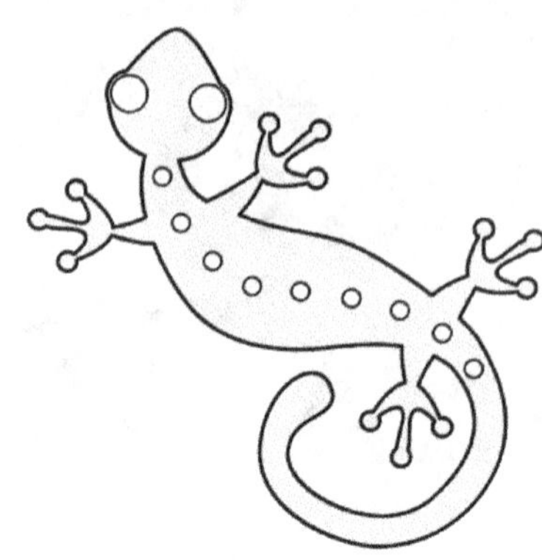

Tracing G, g, G, g

H is for Horse

h is for Horse

h h h h h h

h h h h h h

h h h h h h

h h h h h h

h h h h h h

h h h h h h

h h h h h h

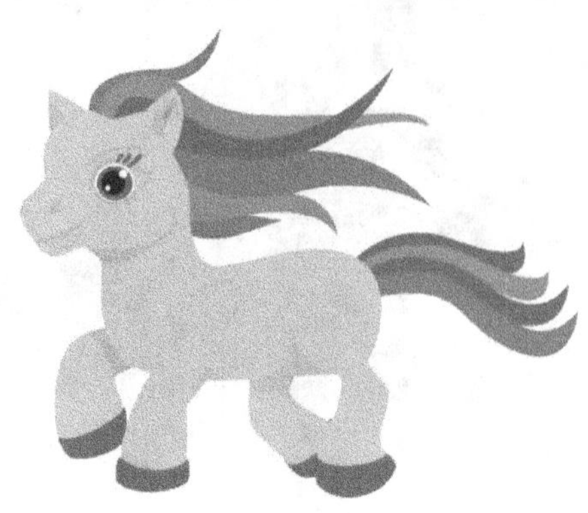

Tracing H, h, H, h

I is for Insect

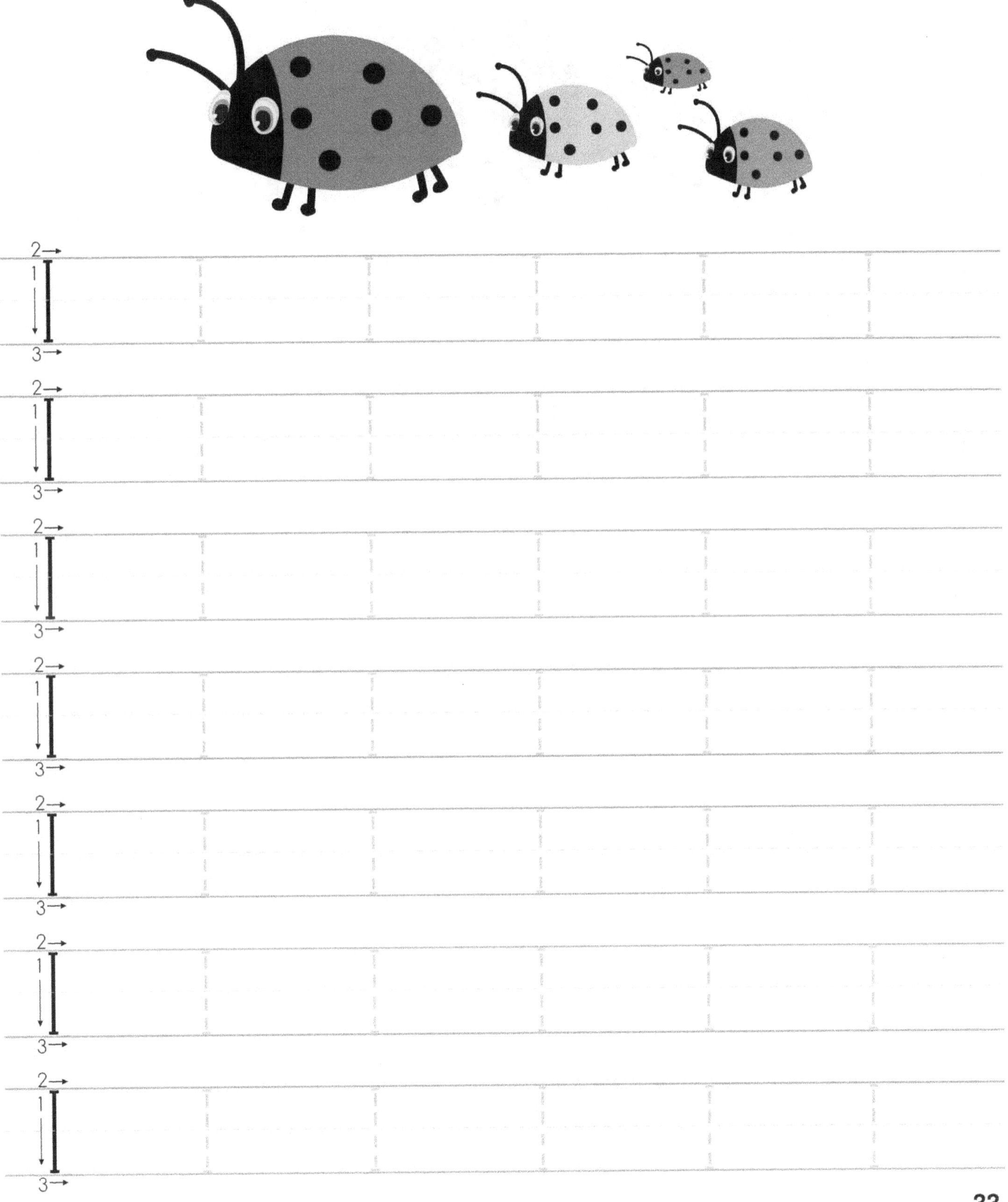

i is for Insect

Tracing I, i, I, i

J is for Jellyfish

j is for Jellyfish

Tracing J, j, J, j

K is for Koala

k is for Koala

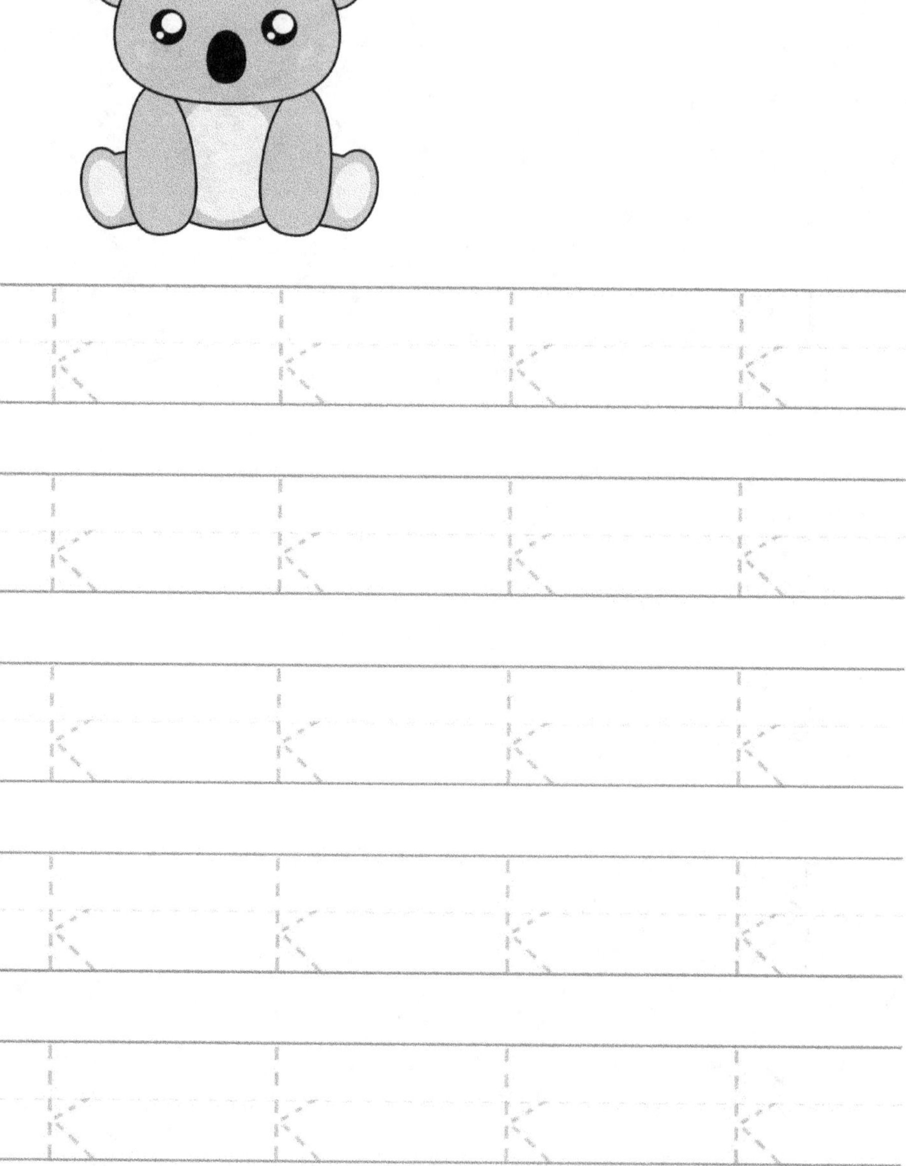

Tracing K, k, K, k

L is for Lobster

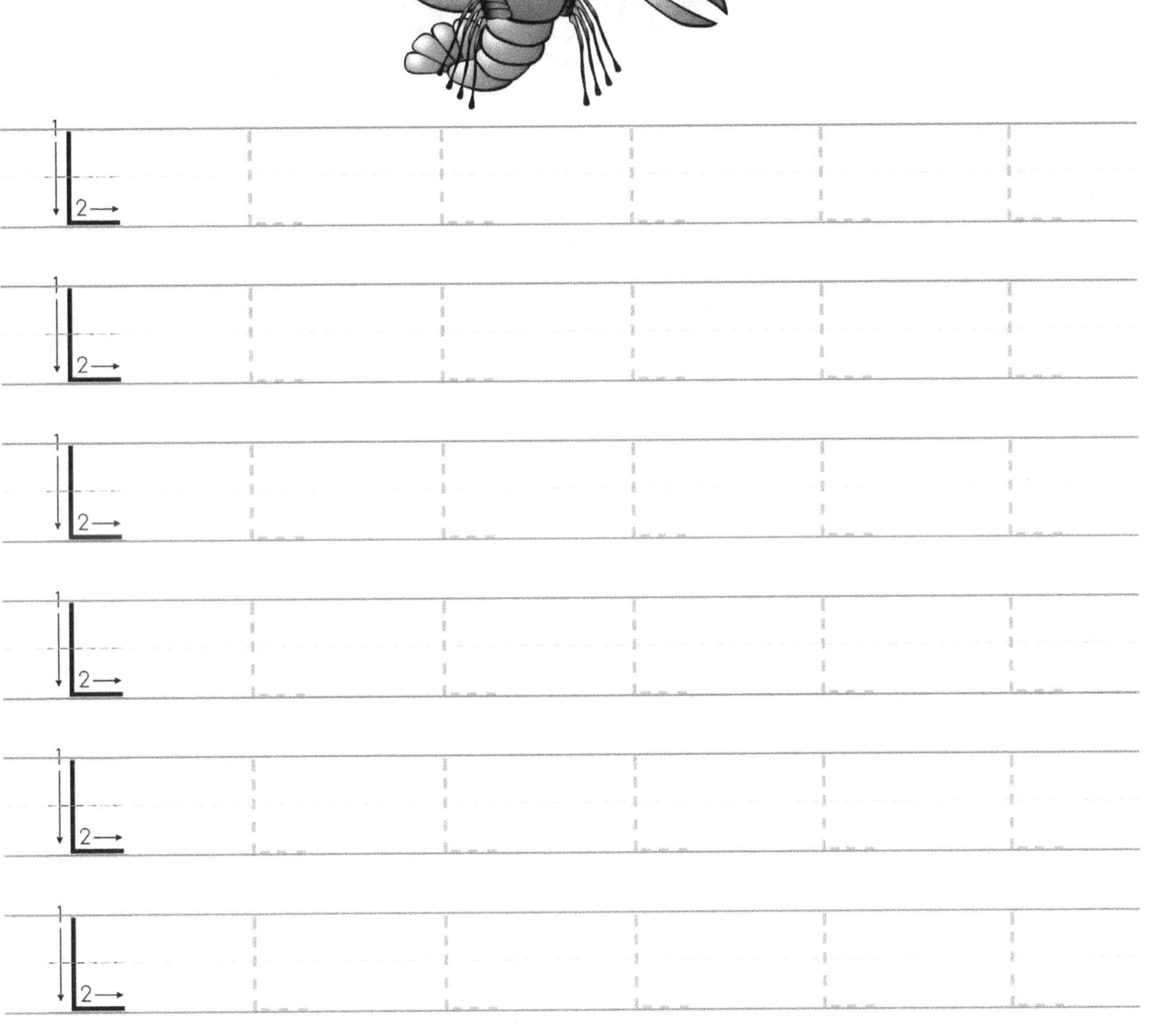

I is for Lobster

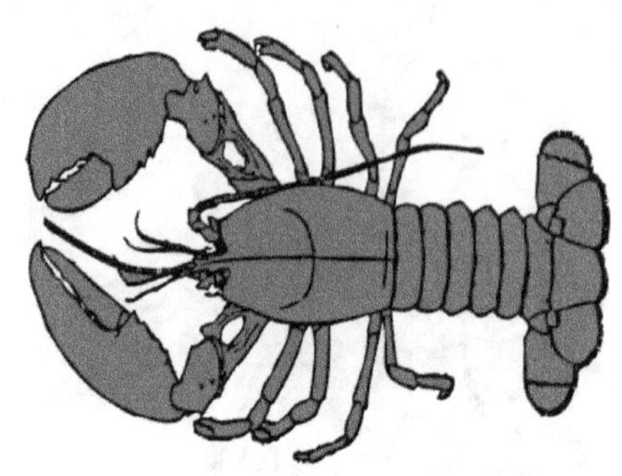

Tracing L, l, L, l

M is for Monkey

m is for Monkey

m m m m m m

m m m m m m

m m m m m m

m m m m m m

m m m m m m

m m m m m m

m m m m m m

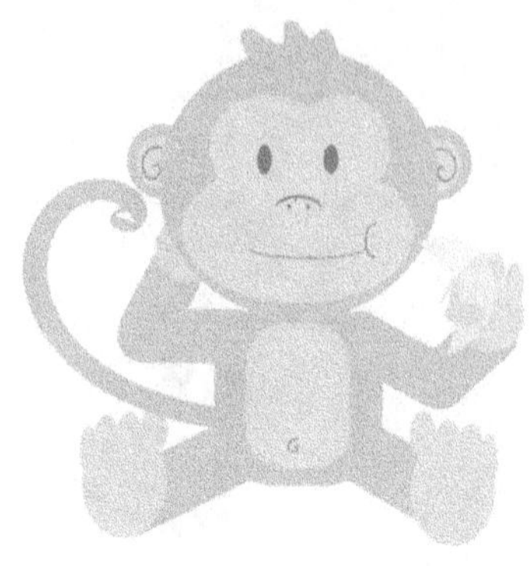

Tracing M, m, M, m

N is for Narwhal

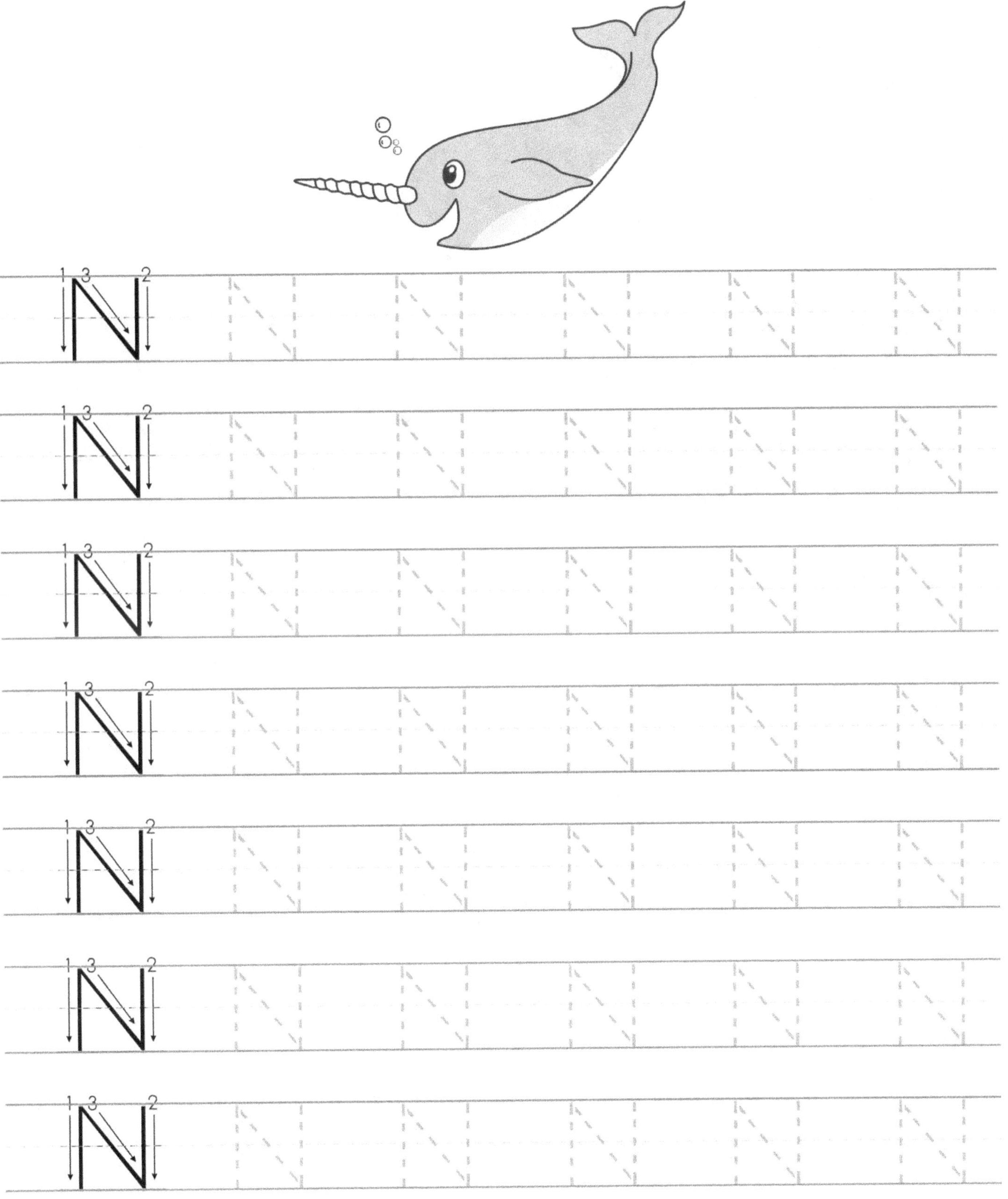

n is for Narwhal

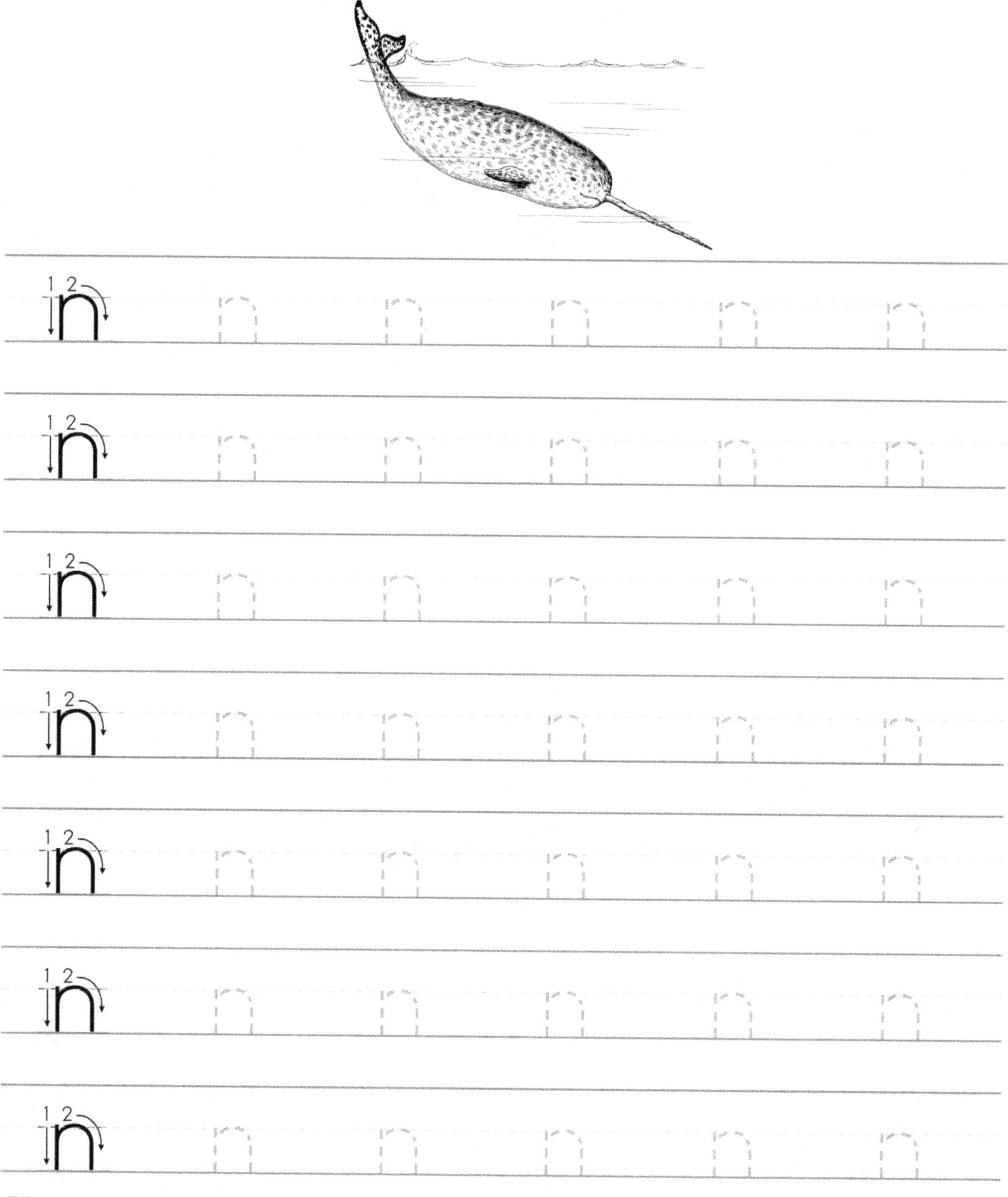

Tracing N, n, N, n

O is for Octopus

o is for Octopus

Tracing O, o, O, o

P is for Penguin

p is for Penguin

Tracing P, p, P, p

Q is for Quail

q is for Quail

Tracing Q, q, Q, q

R is for Raccoon

r is for Raccoon

Tracing R, r, R, r

S is for Seahorse

s is for Seahorse

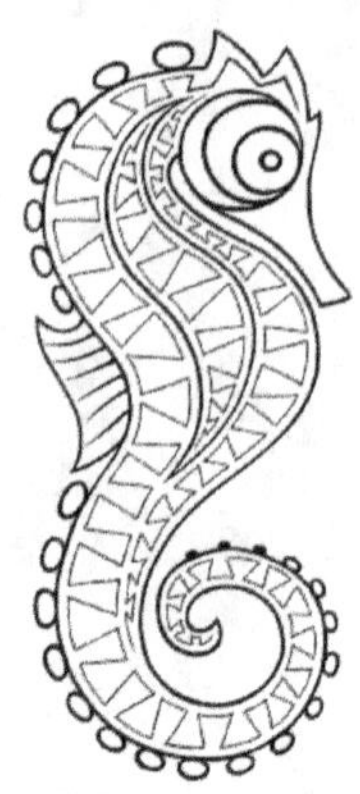

Tracing S, s, S, s

T is for Tiger

t is for Tiger

Tracing T, t, T, t

U is for Unicorn

u is for Unicorn

Tracing U, u, U, u

V is for Vulture

v is for Vulture

1 2
v

1 2
v

1 2
v

1 2
v

1 2
v

1 2
v

1 2
v

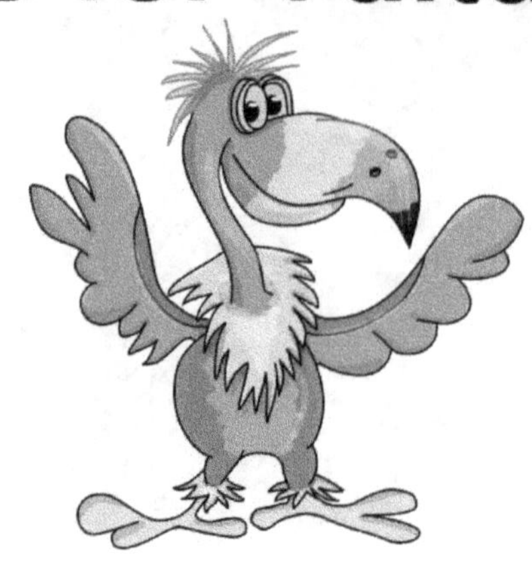

Tracing V, v, V, v

W is for Whale

w is for Whale

Tracing W, w, W, w

X is for X-ray fish

x is for X-ray fish

Tracing X, x, X, x

Y is for Yak

y is for Yak

Tracing Y, y, Y, y

Z is for Zebra

z is for Zebra

Tracing Z, z, Z, z